Nordic Sublime

Nordic Sublime

Matt Haw

Shearsman Books

First published in the United Kingdom in 2026 by
Shearsman Books Ltd
PO Box 4239
Swindon
SN3 9FN

Shearsman Books Ltd Registered Office
30–31 St. James Place, Mangotsfield, Bristol BS16 9JB
(this address not for correspondence)

ISBN 978-1-83738-030-5

CONTENTS

OSLO VARIATIONS

NORDIC SUBLIME

I

In 'Tintern Abbey,' the terror that accompanies Wordsworth's "joyful" sublime transcendence is, of course, history: the bloody presence of the French Revolution [...]. Keats's own related source of terror is mortality; Shelley's terror is foolishness, fear of triviality; as Coleridge's is sanity. We each have our own.

— David Baker, 'The Sublime: Origins and Definitions'

Norway is a land of frozen hostility.

—Andrew Graham-Dixon, *The Art of Scandinavia*

OSLO VARIATIONS

EVERYTHING IN THE WORLD SAID GOETHE CAN BE ENDURED EXCEPT A SUCCESSION OF FINE DAYS

February blued
like steel   like cyanosis

though people spoke
of the potential for spring

in whatever the lark agreed with the linnet
          overheard along the river path

in what the water meant
by continuing to hurry away to its mouth
singing the song of its being

or the bony motions birches made
toward drifts of snowdrops & crocus

all the cold flowers of the season

*

On the high street
the fruit & veg shop was offering
a discount on woody rutabaga—

here's me feeling outwintered
by vegetable matter
which keeps for itself secret stores
                    of warmth & light

Receding snow in the city parks
returned a vision of things as they are

after all silt & sand & water

*

& with them a familiar
                    sense of dread

as with the end of a public holiday
or questions
          of how exactly I plan to endure

even with assurances
                    that a new season
would surely be achieved

& the finely frayed fatigue of living
with winter's constant sense of precarity
migrated in search
                    of new bodies to graze on

In a Pyrrhic celebration
I bought myself a cellophane cone
                    of imported daffodils

in the parking lot spilled rare tears

AFTER OSLO

beginning with a line from Ana Blandiana

Loneliness is a city
                    of scarcely a million

Where everyone is of one another

Where it rains & rains often
each downpour pronouncing
                    the city's name anew

Diversions take you the long way
around endless urban renewal projects

The shops close early

Long evenings are given over
                    to a pursuit
döppels to their gangers

through streets obscured by a lacquer
of grit & impacted snow

*

To live in Loneliness
among its austere lindens
& redwings
is to realise you too
                    are of another

That you'd rather not pay further regard
to the value chain & neither would I

but do care about catching
the front wheel
of your bicycle again in the tramways
blessing the asphalt of Loneliness
        with the skin of your palms

*

At a Sunday flea market you bought
an outdated city guide to Loneliness

among the listings for restaurants
bankrupt these past fifteen years

a previous owner had underlined—

        Hole-in-the-wall noodle bar
        serving Sapporo-style miso ramen
        pot-stickers & edamame

        nothing less   nothing more

        open noon until midnight
        seating at the bar

*

If eating there alone
                late night

you find yourself struggling
to put a name to the familiar

petal-pale face
of your fellow diner
slurping nourishment against Loneliness—

fear not
it is only your image
reflected in the shop-front

The trick is
not to put your trust in the glass

Believe in salt   in the broth

You may yet thrive here

MALE PATTERN

after Steinar Oppstad

There was a tall Scots pine
in the garden of the house I grew up in

rooks nested there

in the oblique sun of summer evenings
the tree
its crosshatch nests

lit up with yolky light

*

Father went out with his chainsaw—

the tree was too near the house he said
one family shouldn't live
                                        so close to another

Then the tree lay in the yard
cut down to its knots & heartwood

& from the dark mess of needles
sharp-sweet pinenes rising in elegy

*

I scoured the brash
found not a feather of the birds

only the derelict nests
mottled flakes of shell
something yellow
seeping into the grass

*

The evening sun
continued to touch my face
my palms
                    the evicted day
with shades of meaning
                                              & so

I took up a fallen nest
wore it as a mummer's mask

went forth from that garden
with little more than a father's lesson
                                            in callous love

& years later
              an inherited chainsaw

FOR OLAV IN ULVIK

> Should T'ao Ch'ien
> come to visit someday, I will
> show him my cherry and apple trees;
> I hope he'll come in the spring
> when they're in bloom. Then we'll sit in the shade
> with a glass of cider, perhaps I'll show him
> a poem – if I can find one he'd like.
> The dragons that blazed across the sky trailing smoke and poison,
> soared more quietly in his day, and more birds sang.
> There's nothing here he would not understand.
>
> —Olav Hauge

In the shade of a willow
                    an absence

You felt certain that a library
& a garden should be enough
to build a life around

I wished the company of a dead stranger
as you did a visit from T'ao Ch'ien

but at your house   at Rossvoll
closed-off sensations
curtains drawn   orchard overgrown
no proffered glass of cider
poet to poet

instead new tenants appearing
from between currant bushes
demanding a fee to look around the gardens

Acquiescing through the apples
a rumour of air was carried on leaves
broad with summer

roving light of your sacred star
settling on high peaks in their white headdresses

ruined farms & gravel pits
with their cast-down rods
                of foxglove & fireweed

scent of warmed pine
which so reminds me of being *away*—

luminous spaces opening up
just so I felt it might be you
                        far out there
on blithe glimmering Hardanger
hauling up mackerel after iridescent mackerel

That brief nimbus of mawkishness
was all my conscience would permit me

It was Saturday so I bought peach candy—

how the colour of the pastilles rang out
with the timbre of late sun
pitched against the upper slopes
                still flecked with snow

In Ulvik I wished your company Olav

There is nothing about me
        you would not understand

LATE SPRING   A RECKONING

A blackened leaf clings
to its tree   some wizened drupe—

the remains bear up
                their utter ruin

In the slow thaw
the soul's ombrometer
measures the current predicament
drop by drop

Nothing wetter than
        rained-on snow

                snow in the rain

                        sleet in your shoes

ON BEING TEMPORARILY IN OSLO

Thinking   just like a poet
about the bare patch of earth beside
the all-night coffee & hotdogs kiosk

where this breezeblock morning
I noticed municipal bulbs
sprouting in spite of

or   *shudder*

because of the spat-out snus
& frozen dog shit
wintered under trampled snow

Nesting birds mocked the bare trees
with twigs & balloon string

the birches
seemed more leafless than ever

When you told me that conversations
about the vast distances between stars
give you vertigo

I'm sorry

I thought less of you
for your inability to credit the sublime
facts of our meaninglessness

but now that familiar sense—
a hollow uplift in my groin

& in my feeble mind also

AUSTERITY FATRAS

I only gather what falls—
hopelessness makes me beautiful

I only gather what falls—
all night my desires are gnawed at within me
by what lives in the grass

As I watch you shovel the year's first snow from the drive
a sense that your world has shrunk to the size of the task
like lovemaking

When I think of the city of Oslo
I resign to embrace it as one might a bitter enemy

I would like to understand why I have fallen
in love with departing—

why hopelessness makes me beautiful

OVERLOOKING A FALL IN THE AKER RIVER

The light of the water as it descends the foss
is milk over slate   like the eyes of the dead
it could be inches deep   it could be fathoms

Great stones unmoving for epochs
line the river bed & sift the light for reason

How it roils

The river is fed by groundwater & a lake
frozen over four months of the year
in a valley high above the city

Were I to dip a hand   the force
would clasp it & the cold it bears
                                        beyond seasons
would set up residence in my bones

That lake provides Oslo its drinking water

                                        O citizens O itinerants—

I fear some small eddy of that cold is already within us

sucking at last year's leaves   causing the blood
to thicken with glacial silts & hereafter

mired in year-round wool for as long
for as long as the river
          spates its course through the city

HAVING WORKED ALL NIGHT AT DAWN THEY WENT TO SWIM IN THE OSLOFJORD

To trade sweat for saltwater

because there can be no puzzling back together
the trays of drinks
that slipped from tired hands

no swallowing the ugly words
exchanged with the barflies
their wearisome quarrels & jealousies
or returning to their owners
the stray bills quietly pocketed

Legacy of citrus rinds
Legacy of beer swill

They swept the broken glass
from the street outside
the dishwasher gurgled
& another night was gone forever
in the stern blue of an Oslo dawn

But this morning tapers
it seems & inclines
        to delicate Christiania—

the iron streets & consonance
& Nail Soup fountain
softened by the city's Danish name
                        & the promise
of a meagre ration of beauty—

the late-shift going to bathe
as the world returns from a brief night's
deliriums & regrettable unions

beginning with gulls' sharp yodelling
a loose grid of contrails overhead

the belt of Venus
an absolving backscattered light

& bodies & bodies & bodies
          leaping into the harbour

THE WEEKENDERS VS FERRY TIMETABLES VS METAPHYSICS

Not a hint of autumn
          though we looked for it

a phone rang & rang
but the impetus was to be away

if leaves fell they were yet green
                 chalk that up to some fungus

& the sea bloomed with jellyfish
suspended in the calm waters
          of the bay like chewed stone fruits

We recalled the previous years
          the mindful business they were

as those waking
from such ludicrous dreams
they betray the fact of their being dreams
even to unconscious minds

The horizon was sepia heat haze
all possible destinations obscured
in meteorological uncertainty

& the harbour we slipped from faded
to rocky shore & the outline

of the clock tower above the rådhus

*

Staying a course between islands
not permanently inhabited
but relevant for their instruction
as to where we were not

we watched the ferry pay out
                    its bridal train of wake

as if what's next might be divined
in the churned waters of our recent past

We talked of the great storms
          that will rinse us to oblivion

or what if the seasons to come
simply continue to flake away
          to delible years & dereliction

like the atlas-pattern of paint
remaindered on a rusted gunwale

*

Imminent cataclysm

The slow creep of collapse

Both eventualities seemed equal
in their ability to blow up
                    warm gusts of anxiety

which led us to think of the helianthus
growing all summer
against our block's south wall

to heights its stem cannot support
without the aid of canes

its head hanging heavy with oily seeds

*

In its adherence to a schedule
the ferry too clings
          to some condition of truth

but at the farthest terminus
                    yet another deserted quay

as if to remind that what happens
happens with or without
                    our weekend souls

salt-lipped on deck smelling
          of exhaust & sunscreen

as far from our lives of the districts
as today's choices allow us to get

& as the pilot brought us in
          as we approached the boat slip
the engines roared their reverse

sending great thunderheads
                    of turbulence rolling
through the clear deep northern waters

more scrying for the heart's glass

& the leaves & the jellies & maybe
some consolable part of the day
                    were lost

PATTERNS WORK BY REPETITION & SO DO I

I wanted to run away with you this morning
as much as I wanted to take you out for falafel

Instead I poured you filter coffee which filled the cup
so monochromatic it was all I could do to keep my hand steady

I wasn't always like this—

    I used to rake leaves
    in an arboretum as vast & misty
    as cinematic representations of memory

    my days like milk poured into water

    in the winter I mulched   forked
    rotting heaps into tree circles

    By summer I was back to raking

    In the evenings I salved myself
    with films about crumpled stoics
    who don't change their lives

    They were so monochromatic

it was all I could do to keep my hand steady
as I poured you coffee until it overflowed the cup

As much as I wanted to take you out for falafel
this morning I wanted to run away with you

FOR THE SAKE OF MY LONGEVITY

You also might learn to pine for a dawn's
fragile arrangements of frost crystals

if only you could miss for long enough
the expansive feeling of cold air in your lungs

For a time I wandered your blued hills
dense with conifers & distance

like any immigrant
with a clear memory of the sun
but underdressed for the weather

Now I grow colder
long nights give me clarity of thought
in a land where trees stand leafless so long
          you worry the freeze took them

I've no choice but to embrace
the wheezy dogma of impermanence—
momentary warmth
swimming an Østmarka tarn

day drawn around me in summer rain
drumming its fills on the lily pads
murmurations of cloud
apparent absence of reflection
                    greened by clear water

I don't want to resort
to making food from sunlight
but neither do I want to make the cold a god

So I'm through with your ways Oslo
        squaring sorrow with a damned sense

walking into the washed-out worldly void
of that same body of water frozen over

Attending to the wind
so easily confused for the ocean

the mournful plucked-glass sounds
an expanse of ice makes when walked upon

THE LIBRARIANS DO WHAT THEY CAN ABOUT MORTALITY

beginning with a line from Elizabeth Bishop

Yesterday brought today so lightly

but it was all a ruse
to make the stamping of books appear
of no great matter to tomorrow

even as the library empties once more
books returned   reservations claimed
elm leaves littering the foyer

A volunteer brings windfall pears
from her garden   dutifully I wash
& clear space for them on the enquiries desk

how they seem to glow from their bowl
even as late afternoon greys the air
        around their persistent ripeness

which is to say
their yesterdays   our yesterdays

I give away as much of the fruit as I can

CYCLING DOWN MARIDALSVEIEN

We agree to ride through the lake
that often forms after heavy rain
around a slow drain
          outside the architectural college

Building up a head of speed
we gleefully watch our tyres
                    parting the water
it sluicing back through the spokes

Pedalling down into all that
biscuit-coloured water
warmed by its rush through the streets

we were delighted & forgot
                    so as to lose something today
another long shift's indignities

the way somebody whistled
or clicked their fingers
          & still you tended to their needs

Downhill charmed
my mind now races into a future
where I almost believe I could love
                    the cycle of sleep & service

each day as alike as the one before
          a procession of children marching
crocodile from their kindergarten to the park

already in their coats
because soon it will be too cold to ride

we will want for other methods
                    of self-preservation

& all over Oslo
rusting bicycles will be chained to railings
their tyres slack & seats missing

O SLOES OH OSLO

We found blackthorn fruiting
in the Ekeberg park
frosted drupes
whose drying bitterness I've known since childhood
        steeped for years to medicinal liqueur

Autumn
new moon sharp as a clipped toenail

We took with us the knowledge
that it was this view over the fjord
                the slow whale of skyline
depicted in *Der Schrei der Natur*

that like Munch
we were both a little tired & sick

Oslo   overdue for snow
for it to mound over parked cars
leave them bound for months
                & close the parks

already the bare trees
stand like gates through which we
are being invited to leave

In an act that felt necessary
I picked a sloe
placed it on your tongue & waited
for your face to wince
                with the astringency

NORDIC SUBLIME

I

ALCES ALCES

In the summer of 2020, the Norwegian press reported that Eurasian elk had been sighted on several of the western islands for the first time in a century.

I trace their route back to the islands
along the mainland peninsula
                to the road bridge at Tysnes

Wilded by the thought of elk migrations
I imagine lying where they lay

on matted lichens & lingonberry
buttoned with ticks
gnawing for sustenance moulted antlers

loving the frost studding the velvet
their palmate forms
        as hands in open prayer to skies
so clear & cold they reassert the difference
                between instinct & want

I've read that elk can seal
their nasal passages when feeding
on aquatic vegetation

a useful adaptation when it comes
to fording the kilometre of firth
one island to the next

This is how I plan to return
                        as in fables
on the back of a bull elk

clambering out on the rocks
by the boathouse where we watched
percussive moonlight play
on water moving through the sound

I will rise in chains of tang & seawater
to lie soaking at your feet

as a lone elk wades
          from the midnight ocean
& vanishes into conifer forest

CROSSING THE POLLEN

Polaris visible   then not
        through swaying pine & curdled cloud

*

I'm hauled by spindrift through the swell
        in a skiff that has sprung a leak

*

Under swaying pine & curdled cloud
with all I care to own packed in the bow
        of the skiff that has sprung a leak

*

I wanted to see the lights
        of the harbour receding
with all I care to own packed in the bow

hauled by spindrift through the swell

*

I wanted this
watching the lights of the harbour receding

*

Polaris visible then not

THE LEAN TIME

You went

before the season
you liked least
could really get going—

the tealights lit
at three   then four
then five

But you missed
the herring nets
being hauled up

woven with shivering
blue fish

Now your jacket
hangs on its hook
in the boathouse
like a gutted cusk

glittering
with scales
from years past

You are not you anymore
& love the spring

have no need
for oilskins
where you are

on the sunlit side
of another island

pulling a long line
from the sea's
green & silent vaults

feeling the weight
of the luckless fish
nipping in your hands

breathless
unwilling to let go

SANKTHANS

At sundown we light the bonfire

that great pile of brash & leaves
as much of the old year as will burn

It's been a dry spring so it goes up
quickly at first   the flames alive
& wild as trapped birds—

later I must help it along   prodding
& replacing the ends of fall-outs
to be sure everything burns

The neighbours come down to watch
smoke blow across the paddock
through thin trees beyond the beck

They stand at a distance
eyes reflecting an ancient revelry

So that's that for another year they say
remarking that now nights
                    will only get longer

then return to their houses
while I rake through spent nails & cinders
sending effervescent sparks into the air

Tonight it will not get dark
                              not fully so

only blue a sudden emptiness
where the fire was heaped

& there the forms of sedges
rickety garden furniture
the house & our lives within

all that we were not yet ready to burn
rising between the ash & dusk

IMAGINING AUGUST

at the dream house
with its seasoned weatherboards
mossed over roof slates

mare's tail & willow herb parting
in the driveway & tomorrow
for quiet company

My hair   my beard
grown long again

The smell of seawater
shrinking my tongue
to the name of the sable bird
chuckling under the goss

all these greens   the cosmos
newly threshed

In love & hungry again
for every ending thing
doubled in the calm
kelp'd waters of the bay

My brimming bowl of ramen

FROM THE INDICES OF HUNGER

The fish I caught was all parts cod

a great sullen beast of the lower waters
                bronze leoparding the silver-green

wrestled from the glacial trough I fished—
a kilometre across & deep enough
                even light goes to drown there

He had a little fight in him
tried to forge under the boat's shadow
just as the pale form became visible
                        in the sea's slate lens

enough that when the time came
I did not hesitate
to get the gaff hook under him
        drag him bodily over the gunwale—

evidence previously disposed of

Gill flaps beat against grey air
sinkhole pupils not used to the light

stared up from the glumly familiar face
barbeled & venerable
        deserving of more respect

It was only the thought of catch-&-release
that flashed then turned in my mind

descended back into the dark
like it too were made of scales

The fish lay there
                    mouthing emptiness

I twisted the hook from his jaw
ribbons of blood congealed
in the bilge slosh at my galoshes

with what passes for mercy
or the flow & trembling of incurable knowledge
as I cut the rakers to bleed him

Fish here they told me again & again
when you can no longer live
on the sustenance provided by song

ON THE TROLL KING'S SUITABILITY AS A FATHER

The way he came clodhopping
round the back of the boathouse this afternoon

reminded me he's made of stone

His brow   his slab shoulders
the three teeth left in his stone mouth
                                        also stone

The rain courses off his chin

The oars of his boat fit
                the hollows of his hands

If he were to lie out in full sun
on the hottest day of the year   I *swear*
                we could fry eggs on his back

I half expect the sprig of heather he's holding
                                        to flower

for a rainbow to arc up
                from slate waters

When he strips his shirt to bathe—
barnacles
        bladderwrack
                the high water mark

The many tides have stained
                                        his fatherly inertia

Just look how the great swells break on him

HEY FUCKFACE

That star you've been sculling toward
is actually a planet

& despite your father's best efforts
to teach you to distinguish
between celestial bodies

we never did quite manage
to make a navigator of you

When your phone slipped
from your pocket

as you watched it sink
its screen light blinking off

you thought it lit up
something pale & gigantic
in the water beneath your dinghy

now it has ceded to darkness

more a part of the sea
          than you can ever hope to be

& that shadow scudding across the sky?

just another oarsman
who can't find his way back to shore

II

THOUGHTS AT TÒRSHAVN

No paradise for we
who have never known home

This agreed
things became simpler

a matter of arranging
on the table set for our absence

a spray of weeds & wildflowers
gathered from cliffs
stubborn with fog

the sad grace of digging in

*

Can we thrive on
what little we need know—

how long it takes
to soft boil a gull's egg

the mineral weight of salt
required to make stockfish

how to chit a potato—

the last oral traditions
itch on our tongues

& grow slack

*

What sort of gods are we?

Even the revenant selves
              we create in our poems
resist the will into being

make our lines little more
than the desperate piping
              of migratory waders

blown here on the way
                          to elsewhere

So we walk the heather
in sleet-rain
or summer's late horizontal light

in our sweat & modesty

inventing reasons why
we should be the ones to survive

as waves iris
the black rocks along the shore

*

If we are going to live this life
we will live it like the Føroyingar—

descend to the bay
where the drive hunt has beached
several hundred pilot whales

We will each take a breath
unsheathe
our scrimshaw-handled knives
& do what must be done

AT MEHAMMAR

No more than stone & fish guts
a drawn-out dusk

no more than seasonal inertia
or being required to abide within cloud

Today there's light enough to turn
the compost
so dark & warm with fermentation
I think of mother's blood

To observe customs without thought
long evenings reading

not books but dated maps
my fingers tracing the line of fells
Grønafjellet   Midtfjellet   Tindane
which Kraken the island

memorising routes of paths
that cross the boggy mountainsides
none now tread
elevations of tarns
        unstirring at my fingertips—

but I need not trouble to imagine it

beyond my window
        by barely controlled degrees
the garden gives over to encroaching
willow scrub & juniper & heather

the wreck of them blown beyond sense
as every night
                    & all

MORE FROM THE INDICES OF HUNGER

What I loved most about gutting the fish
was the initial splitting open of the belly

from anus to chin to reveal
the innards packed in their brine

chrysanthemum of the pyloric caeca
the gobbet heart   the swim bladder
that rapid pressure change
                    had forced into his gullet

it bulged there like a perverted thought
that would not commit to the word

I grasped the entrails entirely & cut them free
with a flick of my knife

From where I worked on the quay
I could hear two oystercatchers
                    harried above the strait

their piping heavy on my ear
with the operational violence
my appetite had loosened from the day's sleet rain

Angling my knife between bone
& the dense pearl-sheened flesh

I broke him down
head   collars   liver   loins   fillets
the trimmings saved for soup & stock

whatever was inedible I cast back
for the iridescent cuckoo wrasse to peck at

There is no accord to be made
                    with the living of this world
when we're hungry we eat & forget the blood
sluiced away with a bucket of seawater

the quick blade & all it severed

A COLD SNAP VS MY DEPENDENCY

Hard light   clear & weighty
we are told it is too cold to snow

the sedges & leafless trees—
          collared with hoarfrost

Above their tops the peaks show
stern inscrutable & self-satisfied
as any Nordic face turned
          to the weather I walk into

Through the woods
temperatures don't rise
                    even during the day

In all seasons it is the wild harmony
          of the forest that overwhelms—

fir & pine & princelike birches
when the wind gets up in them
the persistent momentum of steep streams

Halted entirely by cold
metaphors of what it is to be water
flowing or falling from a height
of twenty metres   break down

Crossing on frozen ebbs
I move to touch the column
of stalled foss

sense hibernation everywhere
the slowed hearts of small mammals
set den-deep   equally unable
to shrug off this dyschronometria

How many nights now have I descended
by the forester's track at dusk
my boots slipping on the same stones—

as to the south Orion climbs up
from the horizon
            into deepening lazuli

SUNDAY BOATS OR A FORM OF ANIMISM ATTEMPTS TO CHARM A BEREAVEMENT

The sand tankers of grief pass
through the narrow strait
between two mountains

emerge into cold sunlight
where the surface of the sea
looks a hammered-out tin mirror

I count the ripples to send
myself back to sleep
where I find you—old seafarer

floating on your back
in this landscape of stone
                    & fathomable water

You have become it seems an island

whose ancient farms
are repurposed as summer houses

their inheritors handline
for crab & mackerel in the summer

where old men
                    salty as you were
still do their evening rounds

to check that the dinghy is tied fast
            in the boathouse

that the lines are in place
the nets hung up

& all the lights are out

*

As bound now to the sea
as poetry to song   neither absent
nor wholly present

but washed by tides
that flood & slack
                    flood & slack

The presence & absence of you
consoles
            or conjures hot tears

a wire held to a flame
          then pressed to the skin

For a moment I can see them—
waves lapping
the corners of your mouth

& reckon that the engines
of Sunday boats must be to you
as the tinnitus that plagues the whale

The illusion passes
the island I imagined you to be
                              is merely that
uninhabited & out of reach

The freighted boats forge on
with their dreary navigations
                                        beyond sight
to what looks like more weather

The repeated V patterns
their bow waves make spread out

among the fabulous maze
                                    of land & water
their forms subject
          to erosion by the light

& where the wake touches shore
it sounds something like loss
                                            like loss

HARD FROST AT STIBAKKEN

The foxed rowan berries

the last of summer's reds
at last gone over

A wrinkled plum falls
an apple   & the jar full

of cigarette ends suspended
in frozen rainwater is held
mid-shear on the table

The air is so clear I can see
for distances that drain
the sky from lungs

to the sun-buttered
peaks of the interior

that seem to call lone birds
in their direction

I thought I too was alone
but this morning footprints

crossing the frozen grass
& later voices in the lane

Does anyone live in the yellow house?

Not a soul

ONLY GRIEF WILL BEND NATURE TO A WILL BEYOND INDIFFERENCE: NOTES ON THE NORDIC SUBLIME WITH MISSING PERSONS

In the rocky verge between the road & the banks of a fjord, the cold has halted the decomposition of the carcass of a young deer. Her blackened coat appears now several sizes too small for her bones. A slack tongue protrudes through the jaw toward the picked & scattered shells of crabs, hollow bones of unidentifiable fowl. In wind & sleet & the strobing blue lights of emergency vehicles, the dead are here to be catalogued.

> *The car turned over on its roof & ended up on the side of the road. By the time the police arrived, it was empty & the driver had disappeared without trace.*

There are many ways this place could kill me; to be picked clean by exposure is just one such way. I am beginning to forget why travellers to western Norway have only praise for the landscape. Their ideas of the sublime frame mountainsides descending to fathoms of dark water, wild trees tossed on seas of cloud. Those who live here know that even on well-lit & maintained roads, we are mortal. On a whim, the land can pitch a car clear over the crash barrier, leave us raptured in the boulder-strewn pastures that flank the E39, at 18:38 on a January evening.

> *The search for the missing driver is ongoing, both on land & at sea. Police, local fire services & volunteers from the Red Cross are all participating in the rescue operation.*

It's true, all the elements of the sublime are here & in the depths of a Nordic winter, I am conducting research into a paper I will never write on the subject. This is because I have never known what it is to be cold and feel it necessary therefore to become intimate with ground frost. I have yet to be tossed upon heaping waters, blown between waves, hugging my knees in the open hold of a skiff inlaid with the scales of fish caught years ago. My instruction by means of solitary terror.

> *This is very demanding terrain, with steep slopes, cliffs, ravines.... It is unpleasant to think that the missing driver could have gone off into this landscape—*

Into the dimensions of nature, into the shrunken size of our power. I draw on diminished stores of manna to journal a list of everything patently alive: Juniper & the few other species of evergreens I can identify; the stoat in her winter colour, a deft white flash along the drystone wall; passerines squabbling for seed at the feeder. Returning from visionary dreariness with wood for the stove, I add myself to the list of the living.

*

Days later the search is resumed. From the picture window, I watch the unfolding neo-noir of Red Cross volunteers tramping through the yard with their dogs & hi-vis. They search the low cliffs on the seaward side of the property, cross the beck & disappear among the stand of birch saplings that mark the boundary of the neighbour's land. Drones hum the looming escarpment. The distant glacier, Hardangerjøkulen, is the only bright thing; it dreams in the midday twilight.

> *There is of course a theoretical possibility that the person concerned is elsewhere or remains hidden.*

The police ask those living alongside the road to check their boats & properties. I search among the hanging nets & tackle in the boat house, the crawlspace above the garage, the derelict forester's hut, expecting to the point of hope to find you dead in each of these places: your pale & bloated form butting against the rocks in the cove where I put the boat in to fish herring; walking the sullen deer paths that cross the mountain, my collie re-emerging from thick scrub, his snout berried with viscera; or sequestered by cold in the bothy above the conifer plantation. Your body no longer your body, any more than it is my body, my body to give language to, my body to declare dead.

> *Based on communications from health professionals, there is a chance for survival. As long as they keep moving this remains a possibility even with the temperature, weather & wind conditions that have prevailed in recent days.*

Since your crash, I've twice read an essay titled, 'The Sublime: Origins and Definitions', but it's my wilderness survival books I return to. I realise now that I know less about the technical aspects of poetry than the various types of improvised shelter, how long the body can last without sustenance, the nutritional value of bitter herbs & species of edible mollusc. I think of Jan Baalsrud, his flight to neutral Sweden, those snowbound months hacking off frost-bitten toes. But there is no consensus as to how long one might hold out in this landscape. I compare a photograph of the Norwegian commando against the image of you released to the press & make up my mind as to who would die of exposure first.

*

> *It has been three weeks since the accident & the young man has still not been found [...] it was decided this week to suspend the search until new information is obtained.*

The last of the volunteer dive teams search an abandoned fish farm. Their dry-suited bodies emerge seal-like from depths of tangled rope dreaded with seagrass. I recall this moment as I later read of the sublime as a sense of personal peril amid cultural ruin. I wonder if it is this that compels me to drive back and forth at speed that same void of lampless highway into which you lately ventured. Witness me crawl from my own wreck. Teach me to vanish into the landscape, or to enter the offices of a local newspaper offering false leads as to my true whereabouts. Will you do this for me if I do it for you?

*

No fowls call, they settle silently for the night. Through the trees, a doe moves. Within her womb the cells that will form another fawn cluster & multiply. She treads through the cold fragrance of wet pine & meltwater. In her burrow, the stoat shifts & sleeps. I desire only my own deep rest. Out in the dark, along the banks of the fjord, there is felt an unknowable mass of water rushing back. Against the weatherboards, the windows & the rocks by the shore, a sleet rain continues to fall.

III

CAROUSEL

What a long winter spent
on a grounded regional transport plane
in a strange northern land

watching squadrons of trucks
with dozer blades heap runway snow
to gateaux outside the terminal

We're in a long queue for de-icing
the omniscient voice of Captain __
I apologise to those of you

living out this winter as strangers
in a northern land

perhaps you're realising
you're not so resilient after all

but you can't now leave the plane
or even get up to relieve the swelling

blimp of pressure in your bladder…

I plugged in my headphones
as blown rags of snow assembled
a blank puzzle on every cabin window

*

Awoke in the reading lamp's pale
drizzle of LED light   it was night

below was a ragged outline of land
veined with the deeper voids of water

the many fjords & glacier lakes
an image of a dream in the process
of being forgotten

Struggling to get my bearings
I turned to the woman next to me
I asked *where are we?*

She replied in a dialect so thick
I wasn't sure at first which language
was being spoken

then realised she was explaining
the process by which stockfish
                                   is reconstituted in lye—

But are we flying south? I asked in English

Avoiding eye contact she reached over
turned off the light above my head
was silent for some time before saying

                    If it is true that the North begins inside
                    it has begun in you & it matters not
                    in which direction you travel

                    for in whichever season we land
                    another hard winter will surely be—

Then the small craft bucked
& we began to descend
through clouds the colour of dirty slush

the kind that persists
                heaped well into spring

AT THE STONE CABIN KNOWN AS TINDASLOTTET

With the warm drystack
of refuge at my back   I watch

two roll-on / roll-off ferries
pass in the summer dusk

distant clusters of lights
on the sea's unified field
simple in their forms
as a child might draw them

each going one of two ways
        both of those leaving

I have lived long in that departing

I believe it saves the world
                from dull love

Apart
with the form of the mountain

the gap-tooth stones of its peak
& slipshod bog cottons

where constant winds play
        their world-shaping songs

some part of me feels arrived
                from everywhere

& momentarily content
to be anywhere but home

This least of me will remain

*

It's not a dream

I have sent you here again
          so late in December
to inhabit this silence

As good a night as any place
to witness the grasses fold
over themselves

to listen
should the stones have
                    anything to say

to see if the wind can name
every one of your bones

for your eyes
to let light in
on this blindfolded hemisphere

a mountain hut within stilled
by the blustering world without

for none of it
to make you think
of any kind of god

Just hang your song
                    with the others
on the hook behind the door—

*

for which there is no key

a wooden bolt   lathed by use
            slides home into its hollow

The soul of any unlocked door says
let others come

to stone-bunk succour
the bothy atop
this whisker-still coastal peak

Let them believe as I do that this
                    all is for them alone

kindling   water purifiers
tobacco in a zip-lock

marked cairns & snipe
                    launching from heather
so they will know they are arrived

Now to sleep
on the shadow-side of the island

NOCTURNE FOR MORE WINTER

The little tongues of meltwater
seem more fluent in the vocabularies of cold
& distance than they were in December—

such a washed-out sibilance of small water
we only half hear its discourse
                    blanketed still by winter ice

walking down through the fir plantation
where for three nights now a tawny owl
has been re-stating her mournful entreaty—

                              who   *who*

Who will take the minutes on how light
                    continues to fail the early afternoon?
when the horizon separates
two subtly distinct abysses—
one grey black
the other all the inky gradients of blue

Past sundown pipes up the owl again

The month's full moon mounts the treeline
doe-eyed & blotchy-sad
                              as she always is

Now let's speak of being enamoured
                              by that which collapses
under the weight of its tragedy—

late winter snowfall   feather-kept promises
the near future

how we thought we could live there
even while some new quarter was beginning
& invoices for our despair were being sent out

crisp white windowed envelopes
                                        stamped URGENT

NOTES

Page 13. 'Loneliness' by Ana Blandiana, trans. Seamus Heaney, *The Translations of Seamus Heaney* (Farrar, Straus and Giroux, 2022).

Page 16. A failed translation of 'Skjærereiret i kveldsola, det brenner' by Steinar Oppstad, *Tavler og bud* (Kolon forlag, 1996); the poem remains indebted to, and is after, Oppstad.

Page 18. 'T'ao Chien' by Olav H. Hauge, trans. Olav Grinde, *Luminous Spaces: Selected Poems and Journals* (White Pine Press, 2016).

Page 18. *Rossvoll* is the name of Hauge's farm in the village of Ulvik.

Page 21. *Snus* is a popular Nordic tobacco product; a wad or small pouch of tobacco is placed between the gum and upper lip.

Page 25. During Danish rule in Norway, Oslo was expanded, modernised, and renamed Christiania after Christian IV of Denmark. The name persisted for more than a century after Norway became a constitutional monarchy with political independence from Denmark. In 1925, it reverted to Oslo.

Page 27. *Rådhus*, Norwegian for town hall (lit. "advice house").

Page 29. 'Via Negativa' by Charles Wright, *A Short History of the Shadow* (Farrar, Straus and Giroux, 2002).

Page 32. *Østmarka* (lit. "the east mark") is a forested region on the outskirts of Oslo.

Page 34. 'Five Flights Up' by Elizabeth Bishop, *Geography III* (Farrar, Straus and Giroux, 1976).

Page 35. 'One Art' Elizabeth Bishop, *Geography III* (Farrar, Straus and Giroux, 1976).

Page 45. *Pollen*, from the Nynorsk *poll*, meaning the arm of a fjord.

Page 46. *Cusk*, a cod-like fish in the Ling family, is often hung to dry in spring.

Page 48. *Sankthans* or *Sankthansaftan* (lit. "Saint John's Eve") is Norway's midsummer festival, often marked by the lighting of bonfires along the foreshore.

Page 59. Stockfish is unsalted, air-dried fish, usually cod or another similar species.

Page 60. *Føroyingar* (lit. the islanders, *oyingar*, of the Faroes, *før/fær*).

Page 63. 'Lyke-Wake Dirge', traditional, *The Oxford Book of English Ballads*, ed. Arthur Quiller-Couch (Oxford University Press, 1910).

Page 72. The title and lines draw on chapters concerning the sublime in David Baker and Ann Townsend (eds.), *Radiant Lyre: Essays on Lyric Poetry* (Graywolf Press, 2007).

Page 72. Italicised sections translate reports of a crash and the driver's subsequent disappearance, as they appeared in the newspaper *Sunnhordland*.

Page 72. The E39 is Norway's major west-coast highway, known for steep terrain, fjord crossings, landslides, and perilous winter driving.

Page 73. *Hardangerjøkulen* is a glacier that lies on the western edge of the Hardangervidda plateau. At its highest point, the glacier reaches elevations of more than 1,800 metres above sea level and is visible from great distances as a low arc of brilliant white rising just above the horizon.

Page 80. 'Epilogue' by Louis MacNeice, *Letters from Iceland* (Faber and Faber, 1938).

Page 85. 'The Moon and the Yew Tree' by Sylvia Plath, *Ariel* (Faber and Faber, 1965).

ACKNOWLEDGEMENTS

My thanks go to the editors of the following publications, in which many of these poems first appeared, often in earlier iterations: *Anthropocene, Bad Lilies, Butcher's Dog, Elsewhere: A Journal of Place, Lighthouse, Long Poem Magazine, The North, Poetry Birmingham Literary Journal, The Rialto, Shearsman, Stand, TriQuarterly* and *Zócalo Public Square.*

I am grateful to my fellow members of The Craft poetry collective, whose insight and generosity have helped shape many of these poems. I am also indebted to my friends, comrades, and mentors Carrie Etter, Paul Farley, Rebecca Goss, Matt Howard, Melissa Lee-Houghton, Laura Blomvall, Isabelle Thompson, Armando Ledezma, Adam Barrett, Tom Kuyken, and Ingrid Stagrum Ottem, each of whom, at various stages, read the manuscript in its entirety, offering invaluable guidance and encouragement when it was most needed. Finally, my love and thanks to Karoline Mehammer who lived this book with me.

www.ingramcontent.com/pod-product-compliance
Ingram Content Group UK Ltd.
Pitfield, Milton Keynes, MK11 3LW, UK
UKHW040344110326
468872UK00001B/764

9 781837 380305